GW00871591

THE TAKEAWAY BIN

The Takeaway Bin

TONI MIROSEVICH

SPUYTEN DUYVIL
New York City

Library of Congress Cataloging-in-Publication Data

Mirosevich, Toni.
The takeaway bin / Toni Mirosevich.
p. cm.
ISBN 978-1-933132-81-5
I. Title.
PS3563.I716T35 2010
811'.54--dc22
2010019800

For Shotsy

Honour Thy Error

In Extremis

Quite Possible (After All)

Acknowledgments
About The Author

The world is bound with secret knots
ATHANASIUS KIRCHER

Oblique Strategies is a card game invented in 1975, by Brian Eno and Peter Schmidt. "Over one hundred worthwhile dilemmas" are printed on a pack of cards and offer a set of possibilities to apply "when a dilemma occurs in a working situation." *The Takeaway Bin* borrows from that concept, presenting poems that reply to various daily dilemmas, specific or obscure.

Honour Thy Error

Lit Crit

Be less critical more often

It's a stitch, isn't it, that there's such an itch
to judge. Critique the gesture, the bad *plié*,

and you critique the dancer, or, as Oprah opined,
when divorcing parents badmouth each other

to the children, the kids' DNA gets criticized.
The road to hell is paved with bad intentions,

thus, a critical faculty, preferably non-tenured,
is hired to make the point: *Accept, accept, accept*

what *is*, except, except, I'd prefer not to. Flip
the phrase: Be *more* critical less often. Turn on

the fire hose of rage, though there's often a kink
in the line and the spray backfires. *You're all wet,*

said the judge, when I criticized his lack of bad
taste. Maybe we should truncate the phrase, stop

while the getting's good. Simply *be* less, emulate
the under-stuffed chair. Let's be less forthright,

have fewer S'mores around the campfire. We're
trying to watch our waste line. A disco diva sings,

*More, more, more, how do you like it, how do you
like your love,* a poetic line, but the new professor,

with so much on the line, hedges, disagrees, then,
judging from our response, calls for stiffer lit crit.

COLOR WHEEL

Use an unacceptable color

Somewhere along the way we left true blue behind.
That and an honest day's work. Duck a L'Orange was

once on the menu but now it's wasabi this and mango
that. Mustard is big. And puce. Whoever thought that

would sell; the odd green color, well, odd. Pink might
prove unacceptable to a man's man but chartreuse is

certain to send him over the edge. I've lost the silver
thread and older needles will not mend this heart of mine.

Beige is the worst—deadly, dull. I need something to
wake me: Tangerine or *Cherries in the Snow* to help

clear the red out (which they tried to do in Tiananmen
Square, banishing the resisters.) Burnt sienna smolders,

chars. I once knew a nurse who wore *eggplant* leather
pants to the Christmas party. Her husband had money,

she wanted us to know. We roasted her later—*did you
see how tight?*—and could have ended up with a fine

baba ganoush but no one brought any pita. Yellow's
been ignored but buttercream has surfaced. I've lost

the thread again. Where did it go? "Unacceptable," cries
the teacher, and hands the poem back with a big red F.

Better choose another career, forget the wine dark sea.

BIRD PECK, WIND WHIP, LIMB RUB

Consult other sources
- *Promising*
- *Unpromising*

There are always consultants to consult for this and that, free advice
for a price, but I don't want to know. If I go seeking I'm sure to find

where the boys are—and the available jobs—outsourced and overseas.
It's a long trek from here to Nepal, via India and the computer help

line. Most give up before the line goes dead, as this one is sure to go,
but if I consult other sources—*Astrology Zone, Psychic Network,*

the falling leaves outside the window, they may fall into my teacup
of a garden, auger something good; my mail order slip coming in.

Another word for consult is *ask.* Employ working man's language;
go on and ask for a leg up, or down, how about a clue? When you

ask you shall retrieve and then you're left with all that information
to sort and file, pick and choose. In the fruit processing plant, we

were trained to be selective as the cherries rolled by, banishing
those with *wind whip, limb rub, bird peck.* I let a rotten apple

through and was fired even though I promised to do better. Like
the kid who penned the note I found on the beach, *I will be good,*

I will be good, written 27 times down the lined page, I fear my
future couldn't look more unpromising.

COURAGE

Make a sudden, destructive, unpredictable action; incorporate

For a covey of robins skewing up their courage to forage again,
the worm turns, the day does not bring dread. They aren't caught

up in existential angst. What's the point? It's hunt, peck and hunt
again. The odds are skewed in their favor, lucky ducks. What pluck

to stare the day in the eye and proceed, to go forth and congregate,
negotiate, find other birds of a feather: aviary brethren. Brook any

impulse towards an isolationist policy. The politicians are babbling
again; onward through the muckrakers and the silt. It takes courage

to face your own demons, the hobgoblins in the mirror. When you
do it's a bromide for the soul and things come bubbling up: the time

you stood up to the bully, the one who shadowed you each day, always
hiding around the next bend. Each afternoon, like clockwork, orange

he pummeled you. Black and blue. Finally, you skewed the pool cue,
chalked it up to fate, and gave him a kick in his hazelnuts; small,

gathered, yet to descend. He hooted like hoot owl and you forged
ahead, never to face that boogeyman again. If you did it in first grade,

do it again. Get out the steel-toe boots. Punt your nemesis through
the goal posts, like a bird, send him flying. Make that extra point.

DIRT

Be Dirty

Be dirty, underhanded. Steal an idea, a plan; steal first, then second
base. The soft lob of the softball takes a wicked dive. The batter's box
is getting smaller and smaller. Your boss, with an unfair advantage,

serves a sermon on the mound, lobs one up near the temple. (If you
cast them out, party pooper, I doubt you'll be invited back.) When
one gets lowdown and dirty, near the baser emotions, it's all who

screwed whom, you'll get yours, three strikes and you're in
it for the short haul. Isn't that what comes before an ethical fall?
You've been done to by someone and it's three sheets and integrity

to the wind. Time to take off the pinafore, get dirty, get even, get
down. (Once, down on the lawn, his body pressed against mine,
my ex got grass stains on his knees. We were going to town and

Lordy, it was fun. Well, less fun than if *he* had been a *she* but it'll
do in a poke.) If you've got the dirt on someone and you throw it,
tell me, who's the dirtball, the thrower or throwee? I washed my

hands of the whole ordeal and though, ethically-speaking, I flirted
with the golden rule, there wasn't a trace of dirt. It was game, set,
and match. In the end, the boss lost his shirt.

THE INCONSISTENCY PRINCIPLE

Balance the consistency principle with the inconsistency principle

Ever consistent I put my pants on three legs at a time. Just like everyone else.
Except the one-legged finch, who, fully ambulatory, clung to his cage with two
feet, only to have a freed rat nibble one leg down to a nub. *Finches, Half Off,*

read the sign on the shop window the next day, but like mortgage rates, the price
had to rise, a feathery inflation of ideals. If asked to imbalance the persistent
principle, the current regime's rules and regs, we'll happily resist the new draft:

no guns, no boots, no service. On *Dallas*, Victoria Principal suffered through
Bobby's fumbling, inconsistent attempts at love. Like a showery dream, who
even remembers the series? Only us in the *Dallas* study group, who met each

week and deconstructed Sue Ellen's trembling lower lip. What did it mean,
her mouth's consistent quiver? Inconsistence lets us off the hook: no one
ever expects the male to arrive, or spring, or justice. Let's balance or at least

question the goosestep of predictability, the same old same old as de rigueur.
Does anyone really believe in the tried and not so true anymore? Once I tried
to walk atop the balance beam in gym class and stubbed my toe which started

a class struggle. I was sent to the school principal who told me there are few
things you count on in this life to remain consistent: love, thievery, and penny
candy to rise and rise, inflatable as a raft.

JUDGE NOT

Ask people to work against their better judgment

Recalcitrant as we are, some good may come of it. Maybe roses in winter, maids in pink. Coffers may unfill and spill on the heads of the more fortunate. Every ill thought will take a U-turn and smite the forehead of the ill-tempered, branding

them for a day or two. It's slavish work but someone has to do it. Asking doesn't mean getting the most desired response. There could be a package in the mailbox, torn, rent and tampered with. Don't we all want to take a peek inside and view

the contents? Later we can apologize with glass beads and drink Manhattans. The days of wine and peonies doesn't quite have the same ring. Judge as ye shall judge but most of us fudge when it comes to doing the right thing. We slip up—

this side of the Mississippi—fall short, and that's the long of it. If we were full of integrity there'd be no room left for a night at the Motel 6 with a six pack. One friend worked out, worked against her better judgment, and developed

a twelve pack. Now *that* was a rack to carry. If you slack off maybe the best judgment is the result. Let's not try so hard to look so good. I know you slipped the guy a mickey, you know I double-dipped. The collection plate was a little light in the loafers as we boozed in the pews. Let the self righteous tally up.

The Worst

Give way to your worst impulse

Our worst impulse has yet to be discovered. There's the usual cavalcade
of stars: sloth, trickery, the catty comment which only yields a surface
wound. Go instead for the jugular; juggle your options like oranges,
give the right away to the cad, the ne'er-do-well, the climber. Stop
saving pennies for the dour. What would happen if you let your Scout
membership lapse? As a still unfurled Camp Fire Girl I tried to collect
beads for good deeds but only ended up with a choker. Fashionable,
but tight. The scoutmaster's daughter had strands and strands, a heavy
necklace to trip over, a jump rope. I wanted to spike her milk and my
impulse cost me three beads, not enough to ring the neck of the ring-
necked pheasant. One impulse gave way to another, but the bluebird
bylaws stopped me from carrying out my crime. *Whereas, whereas,*
I notice, an afterthought, the instruction was to give way to *your* impulse,
not mine, and who knows, your worst may be my best, or vice worse-a.

HONOUR THY ERROR

Honour thy error as hidden intention

Pardon me, I didn't mean to overstep. If it's a question of honor, a damsel in distress, I'll gladly offer recompense. I meant no harm though that's what came a callin'. I cannot guess my ulterior motives but like eternal votives they shine through my every inaction. It well may remain hidden, my love for you—or my enmity—but at some point it will be blundered upon by hook or by crook and then it's all out on the tabula rasa. We might as well unveil the curtain on all our secret thoughts, hurts, they're coming out anyway, barnstorming into the smallest encounter: the grocer who hears about your soul's torture while wrapping up your little package of ground round. Forgive me for I do not know what I blurt, though some of it bears watching. It's not like I don't have enough material; I fumble daily, but it's a lot more fun than never getting my hands on the ball.

GIVEAWAY

Give the game away

The spare socks, the extra toaster. Give the same away to those who least
deserve it; the cheapskates, the two-timers. Double your fun and give away
a secret: you never really wanted fame and fortune, just another piece of toast,
then the next secret, you just lied, then the next; I fathered your baby (even
though I don't have the equipment). Now we're getting somewhere. If we gave
all the games away, the overused Monopoly sets—missing the little Scottie,
the purple card to St. Charles Place—or Parcheesi, we'd lose all our marbles.
If we wait for others to give the game away it may take eons and no one will
remember whose turn is next. There are those with plenty to keep undercover;
there were no weapons of Mass destruction—the chalice and host were in
clear sight, the communion was on the table. If you give it away they can't
take it from you—honesty, integrity, some kind of selfless esteem. Once
I tried to give my heart away but it came back *return t_ _end_r* and I knew
the affair was over even before I got out my decoder ring.

RIFT ZONE

Cut a vital connection

It starts small: a slight, a dig, the weak joke told
at your expense, which creates a rift, as in miffed,
as in *how far we've drifted apart*. The fisted hole
in the wall can't be repaired for to fix the rift is to sift
through the hurt museum, all the trespasses, prior sins.
R as in Rift comes before T as in Trust, and if you can't
come to terms with each other it's time for term limits.
(Incumbents rarely lose.) There's a riff zone which Miles,
lucky stiff, knew and blew, off on a tangent that was mighty
good. Some rifts are repairable; most are not for we are rife
with ennui, and not, as my foreign friend says, *up to sniff*.
A rift is, geologically-speaking, a fault, and while Little
Dorrit said, "It's nobody's fault," post therapy, she sang
a different tune. "Blameless?" she cried. "Few people are."

RE-VERSE

Reverse

Take back the thrust, the parry,
return the foil to the sheath. If
you take back the story, deny it all—
you were never there at midnight,
cocked revolver in hand, your tennis
shoes covered with mud—we're left
to construct a reverse scenario: it was
dawn, there was a kitchen knife, the
gloves were O.J.'s or Mr. Mustard's.
In reverse means we're still in motion,
and by taking it back—the slight or
off putting remark—there's a chance
for reconciliation: an olive branch,
apple branch, bourbon and branch,
take your pick. "Take it back" I said
to my playmate who called me a "butt."
What greater insult than that? Sadly,
in later years, there were more to follow
(same region *and* anatomically correct.)
Reverse means let's bump then grind
to a halt before we persevere. Let's
learn a new pole dance. If this were
better verse I'd worry about line breaks
then revise how you broke my heart.
In your version the chickadees were
singing *de de de* but in my version,
you're always self referential,
singing *do re* me.

Woulda, Coulda, Shoulda

How would you have done it?

With less panache. With the pedal to the metal. With a holy roller.
With her by my side. With a canopy, billowing. With a nutcracker.
(*You're a ballbreaker*, my boss said, without irony). With Irony
and her comely stepsister, Chastity. Chaz Bono had plastic surgery
and I heard he was eating with Alacrity again. They shared
a submarine sandwich. With a torpedo. With my second strike
capabilities. With her by my side, in a sidecar, yelling at the side-
swipe who sideswiped us. With new windshield wipers for a better
view of the playing field. With cantilevers, with torque. With the
yoga instructor's instructions—*Breathe in, say to yourself, "let."
Breathe out, say to yourself "go."* With a blacksmith, a white knight,
a black and tan. With a tam-o'-shanter. The driver of the shuttle van
wore a plaid cap, a tartan skirt. She spoke with a heavy brogue and
called her vehicle the *Van-o'-shanter*. Drive the point home. *Drive*,
said the other passengers, *Drive*, I said, with her by my side. Swipe
the bugs off your grill, smile into the billowing breeze. I woulda,
coulda, shoulda done it differently, if I'd the balls to let go.

STRESS TEST

Don't stress one thing more than another

Don't press or you'll get a stress fracture, in your femur or tibia, your Niña,
Pinta, your Santa Maria. You'll need a splint or spliff if it's been a hard day,

like the lady next door, who has a big green stogie in her mouth by 9 a.m.,
and needs a little something to help her cope with the drama of the soaps.

If you stress one thing over another, that's preferential treatment, and as
my mother was fond of saying, *we all put our pants on one leg at a time.*

She wanted things to be equal between her three daughters, each of us
with the same-sized pat of butter, an equal dollop of jam on our toast,

but millimeters count, size matters, and before we knew it the tectonic
plates were as lopsided as our portions. It's not possible to apply the

carpenter's level to all; the green ball in the viewfinder tilts one way,
then the other. If the Camp Fire Girl's slogan was *Work, Health, Love,*

why did a Puritan ethic get stressed? I had a few beads for my good deeds,
some had more. Janey only focused on *love, love, love,* was knocked up

by the time she reached 13. If the scoutmaster had stressed a balanced
approach Janey would have her figure today, but wouldn't that be a lot

less fun then going overboard in one area, and working around the gear
shift to find a more comfortable position?

IMMACULATA

Change nothing and continue with immaculate consistency

Leave your socks on another day, before you toss them in the wash
and lose your sole mate. Continue to plod along, gather your quarter

horses while ye may. Change nothing about the circuitous track,
forget the shortest distance between A and Z. Instead, find the lost

language: Etruscan, Esperanza; all the letters we never imagined: ^ +().
Keep on keeping on, keep on truckin', hire Orrin Keepnews to produce

your next CD. As a child I took CCD classes at Immaculate Conception
Church and learned about purgatory. *See, see, see the plane*, shouted

the baby-faced actor on *Fantasy Island*. Our jokes, at his expense, were
nothing if not consistent. You don't need to make a grand alteration

to be as immaculately attired as he was in his tiny, dapper white suit.
A little basting around the hem will do. But if your life begins to feel

like a straight jacket, start by taking baby steps, fancy free and sockless,
continue, continue, immaculate as the driven blow. As usual, there are

exceptions that will rule: In the Italian film, *Immaculata and Concetta*,
the lesbian lover puts a bullet to her brain, a sadly consistent story line.

Loud and proud, fifty dykes marched up to the manager and demanded
a refund. *Keep it up, keep it up*, said my swim coach, even though we

weren't wading but drowning. He was insistent and yelled, *Come on,*
tadpoles, hop to! The world is your oyster and the shell is easy to crack!

SECTIONALS

What are the sections sections of: imagine a caterpillar moving

She offered me a section of her blood orange, the Russian way,
a slice of red sunset falling into my palm. *It's sweeter when you
share*, she said, as we sat on the sectional sofa. Around the bend

there's Section 8 housing for those in need of a hand. Late at night
there's always a party started. *If you wouldn't mind, section off
a little piece of that piece of lemon pie*, said my Aunt Marcella,

or the next thought, a new philosophy in bite-sized bits. *I could do
with a slice,* said the homeless man when offered some pizza. He
hadn't eaten in days. What was he trying to tell me? That, like

a caterpillar, we're all made up of sections, each of us connected,
dependent on the next segment of the population to light our way?
If, all together now, we move slowly, surely there will be forward

progress, though it's hard to discern with a naked eye, to see how
the middle of the caterpillar arches up, rises like hope, then slides
back down, moving across the page or the highway, towards our—

or our furry friend's—denouement. It could be the end of the line.
Don't look now, said my lover, as she glanced in the rearview mirror.
There's only one truck comin' down the road but it's a barrelin'.

BUS RIDE

Infinitesimal gradations

Infinite the possibilities at the start of each day: you can wash
the car, write the novel, reach satori if you make the 4:30 bus.

Is it simply a matter of will? The bus, loaded with like souls,
approaches the hill, huffs and puffs up the regrade. To your left

the sun is sinking into the sea. Only in subtle gradations of sunset
do we see the green flash. The green light says *go*, the bus continues,

you hear the person sitting next to you say, "That sideswipe son
of mine, he'll never make the grade." The bus shudders. Will we?

We're fragile as eggs in a carton, some hard-boiled, some a little
cracked. Grade A or double, caged or range free, we're so thin

shelled, the slightest comment sends us reeling. We hash it over
and over, small potatoes compared to what Victor Frankl endured,

then wrote about, in *The Will To Meaning*. He survived the tortures
of the Black Forest, a triumph of will. You can bet when Leni Riefen-

stahl scaled the Dolomites she never took the bus, which now passes
through the Arc de Triomphe and there, in the disabled seat up front,

a woman who looks like Ingrid Bergman, taking a sip from a cup
of coffee as if it's a sweet sip of Calvados. Where would you rather

be than here—this morning, this effort, the infinitesimal gradations
of thought that are, yes, finite, for here we are at the end of the line.

We've made it to the top of the hill, the bottom of the page.

HUMAN FLAW

Humanize something free of error

Is it the human flow or the tragic flaw? Either way it's a blemish
on an otherwise white placket. Every miniscule spot is noticeable
and brings to mind not one, not two, but all our imperfections:
our double trouble duplicities, our less than pleasant lack of
pleasantries. The sad fact is we're sometimes liars, sometimes
cheats, oh heavenly day, let's admit it: To be human is to have
more flaws then a bird dog has flews, so let's elevate our errors,
not banish them: the time you pocketed the extra change from
the checker, knowing full well at the end of the night her till
would be short. Did you picture her adding up the day's receipts
again and again, and still not step up, return that extra fiver?
Or the time you heard the cry for help on the phone machine—
someone needing a ride, an ear to bend, a favor—then lied,
said you never received the call? Admit it: You don't always
think the best of your fellow man, you don't always assume
the best of intentions. When the man sneered, "Go get married,"
as my lover and I strolled queerly by, was it kind to fire back,
"Small minds, small dicks"? Tragic error, especially when he
and his buddy, the fellow riding shotgun with a shotgun, tailed
us home. Go ahead, humanize him, his finger on the trigger,
and the cashier who lied about the total, and you with the fiver
in your pocket, the epithet echoing. Try to make a getaway.

In Extremis

BEAT-NIK

Fill every beat with something

Fill it near the rim, but not all the way. A cup can hold so much,
and so can we. The news is dreadful: wars, pestilence, persistent

folly. But half full we only stand half a chance at redemption,
cries the right, who stand up, sit down, fight, fight, fight every

mother loving minute of the day. Can you imagine? They must
be exhausted, having to fill every beat with something. When is

there ever a moment for a spot of tea or a beat salad? *Beat it,*
someone yelled when the baseball went through the neighbor's

window. No one fessed up, confessed, there was no rest
for the wickedly criminal element. Without the beat, beat, beat

of the tom tom it's doubtful we'll ever get to a deeper under-
standing of who we are and if I were a doubting Thomas

I'd put in for a name change. Why must we fill every beat
with something, no silence or space on the page for a rest stop,

an end stop at the end of the L line? *You bet your boots,*
my father always said, *and then, fool, you'll be shoeless.*

I think it was his *bête noir*, though I can't be sure. I'm just
now learning French, every two franc word I can think of.

He also said if there's some question which way to turn,
left or right, bet on the dark horse; he won't disappoint.

21

LUCKY STIFF

A line has two sides

Someone called me a lucky stiff. It's true. I'm less flexible
than I used to be. *It's my way or the highway,* the country

singer crooned. Stiff isn't the same as rigid, thoughts, spines,
as in *pour me a stiff one,* it's been a long day. After a few

you're loosey goosey, like the baby that fell off a balcony
in the Truffaut film, bounced and survived, as flexible as

Gumby, as Hubert Humphrey, as a salesman trying to make
a deal. Would you buy a used car from the ex-Prez,

who flip flopped as if he'd invented rubber thongs? Now
Nixon was stiff as a bored believer, thought a cloth coat

more flexible than leather. He had it down; *Pat,* he cried,
when it came time to give up the throne. There, in the corner,

was David Eisenhower, smiling that goofy grin, inflexible,
recalcitrant. What did Mamie think? What's the diff
if the party line stays stiff?

QUALIFYING ROUND

Use unqualified people

The fewer credentials the better. Find the most apt to toot
their own bassoon, those whose light never shines under

a bushel; it's dark in there and deadly; mushrooms sprout;
morels with questionable morals. Only the few, the proud,

the obscene know how to pick the under-qualified for they
are all white and pasteurized, though Louis Pasteur wouldn't

have given them the time of day. Who conferred the hood,
the letters, the stamp of disapproval on their worried brows?

(Outsourced and outsized I returned to school to get some
letters after my name. While most pursued a BA, MA, PhD,

I spent my time getting an ABC, NBC, CBS. A PBS was
beyond my grasp but then again I have smaller fish to fry.)

Explicit in the advice is the word "use". It's not *useful* to
gather folks up in a bus and take them nowhere, but like

the Arabian horse trader at the wheel, I'm as unqualified
as they come and, as a Homo sapien—emphasis on the homo—

I think I just might qualify.

FREE BOX

Would anyone want it?

Inside the free box you find the cast offs. An old sweater.
The knickers that were fetching during that brief period

in 1983. A man came into the copy shop where I was
working and asked, "Do you have a gay brother?" It was

those knickers, which wouldn't fit in today's market.
Would anyone want that life again, or the opposite, what's

around the next bend, all that hasn't been minted? New
quarters bring questions about states' rights, state wrongs,

the state ballot. The chads were well hung but less than
supreme. Is it too late to demand a recount? Would anyone

want an instant replay of what we've been given—all this
class division, the cruel subtraction of those we can't do

without? The reverse of supply side economics is the old
math. Soon we'll be counting our blessings on our ten toes,

then—with another downturn in the markets— on one foot.
Count your blessings, crooned Bing, if you're weary and

you can't weep. Maybe he knew a thing or two. Place your
threadbare sorrow in the free box. Let go of that old yarn.

HEROIC APPROACH

Question the heroic approach

The hero doesn't like his approach meddled with. He ordered a sandwich—
yes, a hero sandwich. It came with head cheese and nothing else. Was it

a sign or a slight? Back from the war he was looking for a hero's welcome
but came in through the back door, an unusual approach. No one was there

to greet him, just an empty fridge. So much had changed while he was away.
Didn't anyone use condiments anymore? If you dared question the war ethic

the ex-Prez brought in the National Guard, "On guard," he laughed, then
retreated to his ranch. He liked plenty of dressing on his turkey sandwich—

yes, ranch dressing. If I redeem the coward, I'll be lionized. Then, as Queen
of the Forest, I'll order up a club sandwich and carry a very small stick.

LIE OR LAY

Accept advice

Let sleeping dogs lie; believe the fabricated tale,
that Sparky and Duchess were on their way home,
their car got a flat, the curfew passed, they're sorry,
dog tired, will explain in the morning. Believe the fib,

the ruse, the tall tail, that covers the fact the sniffing
went a bit too far. There was no problem with the car,
no chaperone at the dance. Later, at the pound, there
was a rumble.(The best policy? *Don't bark, don't tell.*)

If sleeping dogs would lay we'd get the lay of the land
or lay preachers on the stump or fireplug, a barky pulpit.
Right wing evangelists speak of hellfire and obedience.
The left counters by claiming all of heaven is off leash.

So let sleeping dogs lie, embellish, let them gild
(or yellow) the lily. My Bonnie dog lies, not lays,
over the ocean. Either way it's a wide, wide sea
and if truth be told we're all in it very, very deep.

BACK UP

Retrace your steps

If we could just back up a little, throw it in reverse, choose
not to round that last corner. If we could spring forward
and fall back, turn back the clock like a person turns a key

to relock Pandora's box, rethink the military advance
as one might turn back an unwanted pass, no whoopee
on the first date. If we could first tread softly then retread,

all the while carrying a small sized stick (we aren't naïve)
or walk backwards in snow, the footwork already laid out,
then I could step back from my defended position and you

from yours, we could unpuff our chests, remove our bullet-
proof vests, find proof there's still hope for a solution. To be
on the safe side we'll back up our disks, our opinions, our

plans, and then plan an alternate route, prevent a tail spin.
Don't get your back up, my mother always says, *or the fur
will fly*, and this is a no fly zone. What if, when someone

spit in your eye you turned the other eyelid and said *Back
at you*, without malice? If Sisyphus could *just do it* in reverse,
walk down the hill, the stone at his back, or if we could read

backwards and this time learn from history, maybe we could
turn the pages back far enough, before the world changed us.

REPS

Emphasize repetitions

I start out the day doing reps, one two, one two.
A push up bra does wonders. What goes around
thumbs around, wants a ride into the next frame

or stanza. There's an urge to continue. "How do cells
know when it's the right time to replicate?" asks
the biologist. Like a Timex, the world just keeps on

ticking, even though it's bruised and battered. We
do not yearn from history, repeating the same folly
again and again. We might as well turn up the volume,

and emphasize the obvious; the mistakes we made
yesterday we will repeat tomorrow, with a slight
variation, if we're lucky. They say it's good to

vary the repeating line in a poem, just slightly, so
the reader won't get bored. Well, we the people
have had enough. At the repertory theater

they mounted one more run of *The Fantastiks*.
It was less so, we tried hard not to remember,
but still kept repeating the same old sad refrain.

ONE DOT

You can only make one dot at a time

The first point of pointillism: place the pen, brush,
crayon on the blank page, make the first dot. After that,

it's begun; the dots begin their timid march, one after
another, forming who knows what. The dot dot dash of

the Morris code depends on the first strike, our capability
to end the cold war, and baby, it's cold outside. If we

sign on the dotted line, well, there goes the family farm,
the workers and lilies in the fields. Poitier had a point;

each plot is sanctified, a precious dot on the map, un-
recognizable but from above. In a prop plane you can

see fences dotting the landscape, the land staked out
and loved. How paltry the pantry if we move too fast,

from plow to super tractor. Slow down, my friend,
a nasty storm is brewing, each leaf a torn dot flying by.

OLD AND IN THE WAY

Use an old idea

Now that we're on the upwards slope, there are only old or older ideas, past their Saturn return. The car's on empty. I've driven my demons out. They wanted some country air. I could dust off the old idea that I'd captain a boat into unknown waters, then again, once I wanted to be a fireman, once a burglar, once a burgher. Ambition's funny that way. I'm without a plan, happily without a man, in the thin of it. The kids are taking out their lap tops, booting up, and I'm still wearing flats. You have to push on to make it to the end stop. It's not the free fall you imagined, something Pushkin never had to worry about. He just let 'er rip. The revolution turned old, a little gray around the Kremlin, but Gorby found a winning recipe before they put him out to pasture. Now Putin's found an old idea to capitalize on. He's putting the beat beat beat back in the borscht.

Easy Breezy

Allow an easement (an easement is the abandonment of a stricture)

Easy breezy, it's cold to the bone out there. I walked the pavement
and down an embankment I fell, like Alice. Her sense of abandonment
was chemically enhanced but why fault her that? The San Andreas Fault
runs smack down the middle of my neighbor's easement making it hard
to get a permit to build up. Permit me to say that I was neighborly, brought
them a cheesy casserole, then sang for my Last Supper. "Now that you
have your supper, now what?" they said. Maybe it always comes down
to what we will and won't allow. The draft set out to make it easier but
I was recalcitrant and balked. As a resister sister I poured blood on draft
files, then spent time in a drafty cell. It can't get stricter than that, a non-
crime and punishment. I stood before the court and asked the judge to
give it to me easy. *Our hearts need a break*, I said, *they beat and beat.* If
they don't ease up, a stricture—or a scripture—will put a stop to this show.

ELABORATE

Always first steps

It was oh so simple at first. Who begat whom, who started it all. But somehow a slight infraction became an infarction, we turned one cheek, then the other, and soon we were spinning, face forward, then butt ugly. *It's a vertiginous life*, said the prophet, a guy who'd lost his footing more than once. Before we could stand upright someone stepped on our knuckles, shove came to shove, and we went ape over the debate, creationism versus crustaceanism. You say you want an evolution, well, we all want to change the world. "He was a cretin," Eve said, after her first date with destiny, "a fumbler, a stumble bum. Whatever happened to the sure-footed approach?" If I say it all began with plankton, you're sure to argue you smell something fishy and that's when the story starts to get elaborate.

THE SEARCH

Once the search is in progress something will be found

Didn't it start long ago, with that first toe dip out of the gene pool
into the bright lights? The powerful hid behind their white masks,
ready to strike, and with a quick slap on the derrière the search
was in progress to find a response. With such small paws how
were we to slap back? If you seek you're sure to find a penny
on the ground. Henny Youngman searched for a comeback line
for his pooch, came up with "Take my leash, please!" but his
wife felt slighted. I find this story line not worth following but
which tail should I pursue? "Once upon a time…" never goes
far enough. "Did you hear the one about…" lacks luster. "You
show me yours and I'll show you mine" might work if you
have a sharp delivery, but isn't there a less slap happy approach?

Tool Time

(Organic) machinery

To get from here to there we need sharp tools—hacksaws,
lawn mowers—that will slice through red tape, duct tape,
the 18 minutes Rosemary Woods nipped out of Nixon's yarn.
To deal with the new skein of fools we want machetes to slice
away the folderol, the excess, like a deli blade slices the ham-
fisted *proscuitto*, paper thin, so we can see through the subterfuge.
Let's trim away the official detritus, delete it, our wheat bread
from their chaff. Everybody needs a tool. Even Mae West,
when meeting Dr. Death, said, "Hey mister, is that a scythe
in your pocket or are you just happy to see me?" She cut
to the chase, made haste, then made love, not war, she didn't
suffocate fools gladly. To get from there to here let's buy
a new shredder or at least paper scissors to trim the dough
around the tin then slice ourselves a bigger piece of the pie.

FORCE

Water

It doesn't help to force it; the lock, the jar, the poem to come
unbidden. Applied pressure is not an applied science. Doctor
Dolittle knew as much, his *Pushmi-pullyu* couldn't be shoved
or cajoled, was anatomically unable to move forward or move back.
Every forced effort is, by its very nature, over the top but there are,
of course, exceptions to the rule: *Smile, Marcella, smile*, is what
a mother yelled as her daughter paraded by on the homecoming float
and Marcella, knock-kneed, intemperate, reared back and forced
a toothy grin. Faced with her mother's iron will, that force of nature,
no wonder she caved. Everyone knows we need to let go and let
God—or some deity—take over, we must not press, but when asked
to go against type our thoughts become weak, wrinkled, in a world
where force is exalted but where might might be wrong. So while
it might be harder to force a camel through the eye of a needle than
the rich doctor into heaven, while no amount of pressure can wrest
water from a stone, minor adjustments can work miracles. A small
yet sharp increase in temperature forces steam through an iron's
tiny little holes.

In Extremis

Go to an extreme; move back to a more comfortable place

If I could slip into something more comfortable; a small raise
in pay, a soupçon of power, an easing away of strictures, large
and small, ignore that the garbage needs to be put out, the bank-
ruptcy dealt with, the troops reassigned, the soul sold to the devil
for market price—I'd be in fine fettle. I'd slip on a pair of slip-ons,
or a pink silk slip and never slip up when speaking to superiors.
The ex-Prez sez: With extreme distress I inform you of the following:
what was is no longer, what will be won't be. It's just a matter
of time. *Move back,* said the cop at the crime scene. He used *Aqua
Velva,* was ultra virile, and so directive! Couldn't he have couched
it in a *please,* or *would you consider*? Either could go a long way
in smoothing relations; ironing out the difficulties, the small but
noticeable wrinkle on the pink silk slip. I'm more comfortable now
that I've got that off my hair vest, but if you look close there's
still an unsightly hot spot on the world's worn placket.

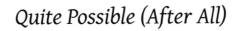

Quite Possible (After All)

THE WAYWARD COURSE

Courage!

Cast away the cloak of fear, all that hinders, unencumber.
Leave behind all mother doubt, fear is not a gift but weights,
the gown is leaded at the hem. Did Hoffa sink below the Thames
or was it the East River? Question what is handed down, de-
construct, then sand it down, a wedding dress, with hooks and
stays, a safety pin that pricks. (You say I do, then reconsider.)
Toss aside the roof, the joists, the rafters, how a house confines,
walls with lead like x-ray vests, heavy on a smallish chest, offer
no protection. Sweep the darkened closet clean: of moon boots,
bow ties, leisure wear, the red snowsuit of worries, cares, all garb
in which you cannot move. If you leave the pier behind and with
it every fear behind, swim without a suit or cap, fins or goggles,
naked laps, you'll shimmer in your gay apparel, with your form
I have no quarrel, we'll set out on a wayward course.

LOVE BOAT

Ask your body

Hurry past prehensile toes and non-prehensile ankle bones.
Give a peek at capillaries; below the skin it's statutory.
I see Paris, I see France, when you banish underpants
but give me L.A., give me Texas, just below the solar plexus.
Once inside the heart or lungs or pancreas—those Dharma Bums
who never did amount to much—I'll apply my tender touch,
will Elmer's Glue your vertebrae, fuse the spine, stop the sway,
squash the blossom, paint the lead, slip into the Murphy bed.
If you let me under skin, we'll make a different kind of sin,
a hoot, a holler, slightly sleazy, but it makes me feel so breezy,
and I'll know you inside out, fuck decorum, twist and shout.

If our interest goes below the surface plane then love will grow.
We'll deepen thus our bond.

THE LEDGER

Simple subtraction

What if our knowledge extended beyond the finer points
to the blunt cut, the bruise in the pear? If you can get over
the dog you can get over the tail, short stubby thing or long
feathered one which brings other possibilities. We edge a little
forward each day, or back, crest at some news, then banish friends.
After I read *Heidi* I wanted to drink my milk from a wooden bowl.
The Swiss Alps didn't materialize, the crippled one in the chair.
What shall we do with the truly phlegmatic? Bake your chest out
said Dr. Westover, who died of a chill. I've done my best to attract
birds, bought suet, bells of seed. I've made it pleasant for them.
We minister to the sick on our off days but like waves they spill over.
The more fortunate are forever with us: fat, happy, and sanguine.

If they took this world away then we'd all be bereft. Or fail trying.
Each little sin is recorded, don't you know, and the ledger is thick.

PERSIST

Just carry on

Even though it would be nice, wouldn't it, to go buck-naked
into the world, shed snakeskin, second skin, but never second sight,
it's still unfathomable, isn't it, the degree we need to let go of the past,
to dress down. There are veils and shadows and shadow puppets
in the firelight glow, someone's hands all over the strings, ghosts
who manipulate (darling, will you steer?) and a story—classic, long
overdue—is projected on the screen: good and evil spring from
the same source, a heart of gold is tarnished, someone gets their
comeuppance, life treads on. The past is clearly no longer of use—
last year's model, the old prosthesis, the circle pin—yet what is no
longer serviceable still persists, like a cough, or a mangle. (We need
some days to make things thin.) Let's then, for a moment, let the old
wall heater kick in and warm our backsides with this spanked heat.

FORECAST

Go outside. Shut the door

CL. As a pane of glass. As your intentions. A low pressure system. ("If you think about it, dear, can you pick up some milk?") He felt his arthritis acting up, a hitch in his gate, like a latch key kid. On the coast there are posted small craft warnings ("Let's decorate Clorox bottles!") *Oh the wayward wind, is a restless wind.* They tell me it's a WN WN situation. The sea level barometer reads 30.7. It's a game of inches. You know what they say: big boots, big forecast. Record low (after the divorce). Record high (when she kissed me). "...in the south-west after sunset. There is another planet here, one that is not visible without optical aid, Uranus. More tomorrow." Later today, a storm will move in, a cold front. Then, if we admit our wrongdoing, partial clearing. If not, let it SN, let it SN, let it SN.

NORTH AND SOUTH

It is quite possible (after all)

If you try to structure pleasure it's quite possible
the day will turn on a dime or, if our moments
are devalued, a nickel. If the sky caves our path
may be shortened from a 12K to a 10. There'll
be less time for a stolen kiss with a stolen miss.
Why this plaster cast on our erotic movement?
There shouldn't be any equivocating; no equator
line across our hot spots, a demarcation to separate
the heady north from the lusty south. *Forget? Well...*
sayeth the New South, *let me think about it.* It's
quite possible I'll find my way to the unpromised
land if I put this pen down, cross the finish line,
and receive what the day offers: fritters and grits
or a stud muffin—perfect in itself, after all.

ABANDONMENT ISSUES

Abandon normal instruments

Abandon the gas gauge, front page, egg beater, two-seater, skill saw, the great maw of the sea. Abandon the forceps, instead of pork, try tri-tips. (This little piggie, bored to tears, cried *en oui oui oui* all the way home.) The abandoned car was missing a jack so Jill thumbed a ride to Normal, Illinois. There is such a place; a town missing a wanton sense of abandon, each won ton wrapped a little too tight. Bandon Beach, Oregon, is nice for a one nighter, the crashing surf and turf. "You're abnormal" said my personal trainer after she measured my peccadillo, then my body fat. I threw out her scale, along with the calculator, typewriter, the hi-fi, the low. In Kentucky, they tossed washing machines down the holler and the stage was set for another coal miner's daughter. Jill took up her guitar—an abandoned star—then climbed back up the hill.

HOMEGROUND

Use filters

Get within any proximity of home and they sniff you out—
a family's pheromones stronger than anything *Chanel*
could produce. Lower the lampshade on the drama, filter
out the sediment, the sentiments: long rows of sorrow
ready for harvest once again. How does a person rewrite
the past? In the dream I yelled "I'm free," only to wake
up in a sweat. Suit yourself, said the therapist, but at least
filter out the static, then cling to what you know to be true.
(*Cling*, I replied, *that's what they do!*) In the used filter all
that's left are the home-grounds; sodden, clumped together,
like family. The strongest brew.

LIMBER

Bridges
- *build*
- *burn*

What we need is greater flexibility. The man
called the human pretzel contorts into a square
knot, a box kite, a pyramid, as limber as Gumby
but less green. When you're inflexible, out on
a limb with your relations—*I love you, I love you
but leave me alone*—that limbo makes everyone
unhappy, frozen solid like the Yukon in winter,
before the thaw. *When you said goodbye I thought
my heart would melt.* Why not place yourself
on the periphery, in the liminal position? Go find
a larger range of motion. If you're still bruised up,
buttercup, out of plum, or some other fruit, send
a shoot out to a new branch of the family. Blood
is thick and should matter.

HEATHCLIFF

Ghost echoes

Out here, on the white cliffs, with my collar turned up,
then turned down. There's a tree. Then no tree. A golden
hillside a minute ago. Now, a white wall. Mirage or oasis?
Panorama or a bad bit of beef? The car lights only go so far,
our vision even less. Forget permanence: the fog giveth
and the fog taketh away. Rail against the dying of the light,
just don't fuck it up for everyone. Was that how it went?
There's a fig tree. Now it's gone. A child in the street.
Gone too. We all want lessons in detachment. We think
that will make us care less. Let me make it easy for you:
I'm coming over. Or I'm not.

THE QUIET ZONE

Don't break the silence

No one told the bird dogs. Their eagle eyes spot the morning
dove and they start up. A neighbor yells out "noise pollution!"
and before you can say Jiminy Cricket someone else joins in
to pollute the argument. "You're polluted," she said to her hubby
when he returned from the bar with six pints in him. She'd been
fuming in silence on the couch, waiting for the big shebang
which never came. The neighbor calls for her orange tabby, *Fluffy,*
Fluffy, and when that doesn't work, screams, *Fluffy, you prick!*
and the holy night is broken. Two blocks over a cat fight breaks
out and the dogs start up again, birdless but vocal. They're primed
for anyone breaking and entering but what do we have of value?
Our earthly treasures, just someone else's dog bones. Silence is
golden, that's what they say, you can take that to the bank, yet
all he was looking for was a break, a chance to vault this life
full of hits and misses, full of what's his and what's the Missus.
Once she was his lovey dovey. Now she yells, *That's the last time*
I wait up for you. Evening crickets start up and he's on the couch
again, a thin dog blanket for cover, not very fluffy after all.

ORDERLY

Look at the order in which you do things

There's the cat to be put out. First thing. Though there is no cat.
I pour an imaginary bowl of milk, pet the cat's nonexistent fur,
call Scotland Yard to file a missing person's report while missing
some key information—who am I looking for? I look at the day
before me, see it's a *come as you are* party; the neighborhood
ladies in various states of undress. "You caught me with my pants
down," someone says, and I say, "Let's get this party started, fore-
stall the regular order of things; putting the coffee on, bonking
the milkman, sliding into suburban oblivion." If there's no wicked
picket fence, no kids, no husband, we can order up some ham and
eggs or a new scenario: the sun was shining on Anapurna this morning,
the upper slopes (*this life, an upwards slope*, says the cat). A sherpa,
on his day off, wanted to reverse the order, put his feet up, trekkers
at his beck and call, hamstrung in their hamstrings. The milkman,
pulling up his pants cried out, *Look at the order in which you do
things*! but the Dalai Lama replied, "To escape the karmic wheel
don't do do do what you've done done done before."

REMIX

The tape is now the music

What did you miss the first time? The knot
in the rope, knot in the stomach, note
on the fridge, *send cash quick*? Not a good
sign from the young pup trying to make his
way in the world. He still needs an allowance
as do we. Permit us to return the way we came.
To retrace you must learn to trace the outline
of mystery. Whodunnit? A chalk line around
a fallen body isn't hard to master. Just follow
the border, not the border fence, in our home
of the free. With my free hand I drew open
the fridge, took out a piece of cake, some milk,
as cold as if it spent the night in the morgue.
Are we past our due date? Find the dotted line
you forgot to sign. X marks the spot of the crime,
seen or missed. *Where is the love*, sang Roberta
who caught flack for the remix. She was killing
me softly with her song but no one seemed to
care when someone left my cake out in the rain.
With luck I'll never have this memory again.

FREE

Lost in useless territory

Free to be you and
ennui sets in, when you
least expect it. All is lost:
the game plan, floor plan,
what you were planning
to wear to the ball. How
temporal was my valley,
is what the actress should
have said, yet something tells
me it's all happening at the
gym; that's where you'll
find the plodders, planners,
the fillies of the field. You
can sink your head in the
strand or swim but first,
try to remember a callow
fellow. If you remember,
then burrow.

HOLEY, HOLEY, HOLEY

Do we need holes?

How else for the flow to flow through? We need the standard bearers—
the ENT ports, drip spots, the disposal, the sockets and outlets of sexual
desire, and holes less noticeable but as necessary: the opening around
the heart, the attic window of the third eye. Some have more, some less.
Jesus needed extra openings, so voilà, the stigmata! Holes still have
a bad rep, as if something's lacking. Before you know it the road crew
is called in, asphalt at the ready. Isn't it better for the wheel to find the
pothole, to be jolted awake? Otherwise we ride blithely down the road,
oblivious to the falling leaf, the triple rainbow, the four point buck on
the periphery. Let perforate daily, poke holes in the social fabric or else,
like Sartre, there'll be no exit for all we contain. If the thought leaves you
feeling punch drunk or even stranger, you can always cut your losses,
downsize to a hole in one.

LANDFILL

Discard an axiom

Look before you leap. Let's toss that one. Jump blindly
into the fold between the sheets, 500 count but who's
counting? You're such a stitch, sayeth the happy home-
maker, who was embroidering the truth about her less
than happy home. *Om, om, oh the range!* chanted Ginsberg,
his axiom while he spun on his axis. Lennon asked us
to *imagine*, imagine that, while Yoko's ax, "life/death,
life/death," was catchy but got a little repetitive. Let's
break the cycle. It's never either or. Either way is fine
by me. If we toss out all the axioms imagine the landfill
problem. Who'll cart them off to sea and dump them
where the sun don't shine? Discard that smirk, young
fella, or we'll card you at the door, and he replies, wise
behind his ears, *Why not toss the card, forget the oblique
strategy? Let bygones be bygones, let's be friends again.*

THE TAKEAWAY BIN

Take away the elements in order of apparent nonimportance

Toss out any crummy little ax to grind. The wood's chopped.
You have enough for the long cold winter ahead. Take away
what you planned to do today: trim your nails, build a seesaw,
sweep the ocean floor. It's less important to get the worm
than to have one last frame of the dream; you were climbing
a mountain. At the summit was a café called *Happiness*.
Inside, in a glowing golden room, people were, yes, happy,
quietly sipping their cups of tea. It wasn't important who
did what to whom, yesterday's knife in the back. The blade
wasn't sharp, your wit less so. Before she takes your order
the waitress points out the daily specials on the blackboard,
then tells you to leave what you don't need by the door. In
the takeaway bin. Your worries. Fears. The go go boots that
never fit. The knitted scarves received as gifts, *veils over your
eyes*, she says. Take away the elements of your unhappiness,
then the elements themselves, five, when we last counted, or
was it four? Fire, water, earth, oh, air it out. She hands you
a cup of tea. "Now, you're ready," she says. "Get out of bed.
The day lies before you, clean as a slate. It's yours to write on."

ACKNOWLEDGMENTS

A deep debt of gratitude to the following for their ongoing support and encouragement over time: Kathy Fagan, Jim Elledge, Carol Brewer and Linda Trunzo, Marny Hall, the Girls in the Shed, Tod Thilleman and Nava Renek of Spuyten Duyvil Press, fellow travelers at the MacDowell Colony, Djerassi Resident Artists Colony, Espy Literary Foundation, and Blue Mountain Center, and Shotsy Faust, whose keen literary eye sharpens all my work and whose humor and heart fills my days.

I also wish to thank the editors of *My Oblique Strategies* (Thorngate Road Press) and *Queer Street* (Custom Words) in which some of these poems first appeared and additional thanks to the editors of the followiing literary journals: *Eleven Eleven, 5 A.M., Fourteen Hills, Gay and Lesbian Review, Hunger Mountain, The Journal, Lodestar Quarterly, Poetrymagazine.com, Speakeasy, The Bark, The Laurel Review.*

ABOUT THE AUTHOR

Toni Mirosevich is the author of a book of nonfiction stores, *Pink Harvest* (Mid-List Press, First Series in Creative Nonfiction Award, 2007 Lambda Literary Award Finalist), three collections of poetry, *My Oblique Stategies* (Thorngate Road Press, Frank O'Hara Chapbook Award), *Queer Street* (Custom Words), *The Rooms We Make Our Own* (Firebrand Books) and co-author of *Trio: Toni Mirosevich, Charlotte Muse, Edward Smallfield* (Specter Press). Her multi-genre work has been anthologized in *The Best of the Bellevue Literary Review*, *Best American Travel Writing*, *The Gastronomica Reader*, *The Impossible Will Take a Little While*, *The Discovery of Poetry* and has appeared in *Kenyon Review*, *The Journal*, *Zyzzyva*, *Five Fingers Review*, *Puerto del Sol* and other publications. She has been awarded fellowships with the MacDowell Colony, Blue Mountain Center, Djerassi Resident Artists Program, and Espy Literary Foundation, was recipient of the Astraea Foundation Emerging Lesbian Writer in Fiction Award, and has received multiple Pushcart Prize nominations. She is a Professor of Creative Writing at San Francisco State University, and former Associate Director of the Poetry Center and American Poetry Archives. She lives with her wife, Shotsy Faust, in Pacifica, California.   WWW.TONIMIROSEVICH.COM

SPUYTEN DUYVIL
Meeting Eyes Bindery
Triton